Everyday FAMILY Meals

There's a great deal of nostalgia for honest-to-goodness family cooking: hearty soups, slow-cooked stews and satisfying roast dinners, complete with Yorkshire pudding and an array of fresh vegetables. Grown men in city suits yearn for the puddings that Grandma used to make – creamy rice, crisp-topped apple crumble and bread-and-butter-pudding, while children raised on fish fingers and chips followed by instant whip don't know what they've been missing.

Everyday Family Meals *includes all the old favourites, but because we live in an era where the cooking is likely to be shared by the whole family, and time is often a commodity more sought after than rare spices, the book also contains plenty of ideas for speedy snacks, salads both simple and sumptuous, and recipes for pasta and pizzas that can be made at home in less time than it takes to telephone for a takeaway.*

We all aim to eat less meat and more fresh fruit and vegetables, but it isn't always easy to persuade the family to eat up their greens. The first step to a solution is provided by the chapter on vegetables, where convenience foods are combined with fresh produce to provide a mouthwatering selection of side dishes.

CONTENTS

SHORT ORDER CHEF

Good fast food for all the family - that's the aim of this opening chapter. Omelettes, practical pasta dishes and quick pizzas, plus more sophisticated but equally speedy snacks mean that you need never be short of a short order recipe.

Asparagus Omelette

2 eggs

1 tblspn water

1 tspn melted butter

3 drained canned asparagus spears

1 Warm an omelette pan over very low heat.

2 Lightly mix the eggs and water in a bowl. Brush the pan with butter, raise heat and pour the egg mixture into the pan. Tip the pan so that the mixture coats it evenly.

3 Gently drag the uncooked egg mixture to the centre with a spatula as the omelette starts to set, allowing uncooked mixture to flow to the edges.

4 When the top of the omelette is set, place the asparagus spears across the centre. Flip the outer edges over in turn to cover the asparagus. Using the spatula, slide the omelette onto a serving place. Serve immediately.

Serves 1

Tomato Salad

6 ripe tomatoes

1 tblspn chopped fresh basil

1 tblspn red wine vinegar

2 tblspn finely chopped fresh parsley

Dressing

60ml (2fl oz) French dressing

60ml (2fl oz) mayonnaise

1 Slice the tomatoes thinly and evenly. Arrange in concentric circles on a plate.

2 Combine the basil and vinegar in a small bowl. Spoon over the tomatoes. Sprinkle the parsley over the top.

3 Whisk the French dressing and mayonnaise together in a jug, pour over the tomatoes and serve.

Serves 4

Smoked Cod and Blue Cheese Frittata

6 eggs, lightly beaten

250ml (8fl oz) single cream

60g (2oz) blue cheese, crumbled

1 red pepper, finely chopped

1 tblspn snipped chives

2 tblspn finely chopped fresh dill

250g (8oz) smoked haddock, skinned and cut into 1cm (1/2in) cubes

1 Preheat oven to 180°C (350°F/ Gas 4).Combine the eggs, cream and blue cheese in a large bowl; mix until well combined. Stir in the chopped red pepper, chives, dill and smoked haddock. Mix well.

2 Pour the mixture into a greased 23cm (9in) flan dish. Bake for 30 minutes.

Serves 4

Tomato Salad, Asparagus Omelette

Prosciutto Pizzas

Spaghetti with Pesto

60g (2oz) fresh basil leaves, plus basil sprigs for garnish

3 tblspn pine nuts

4 cloves garlic, crushed

1/2 tspn sugar

1/2 tspn salt

5 tblspn mild olive oil

375g (12oz) spaghetti

1 Combine basil, pine nuts, garlic, sugar and salt in a blender or food processor. Process briefly to mix. With motor running, gradually add oil through lid or feeder tube, as when making mayonnaise. The mixture will form a thick sauce. Scrape pesto into a bowl or jug, cover and set aside.

2 Bring a large saucepan of lightly salted water to the boil. Add spaghetti and cook until just tender.

3 Drain spaghetti and tip it into a heated bowl. Add pesto and toss until all the spaghetti is evenly coated. Serve at once, garnished with fresh basil.

Serves 6

Spaghetti with Pesto

Prosciutto Pizzas

2 crusty bread rolls, cut in half

3 tblspn tomato purée

8 small slices prosciutto

4 slices mozzarella cheese, 5mm (3/4in) thick

2 tblspn finely chopped red pepper

2 tblspn chopped fresh parsley

1 Preheat oven to 180°C (350°F/ Gas 4). Spread each half roll with tomato purée. Top with two slices of prosciutto, then add cheese. Combine red pepper and parsley in a small bowl and sprinkle a quarter of mixture over each roll.

2 Arrange rolls on a baking sheet. Bake for 10 minutes or until cheese has melted. Serve at once.

Serves 4

Variations
Pitta pizzas: Slit small pitta breads in half through the middle. Arrange on baking sheets with the soft bread uppermost. Top as suggested above or with thinly sliced tomatoes, onions and crisp fried bacon. Omit the mozzarella; sprinkle with grated Cheddar cheese instead. Bake as suggested above.

Tomato Chilli Beans

250g (8oz) red kidney beans, soaked overnight in water to cover

1 tblspn oil

2 onions, chopped

1 green pepper, chopped

2 cloves garlic, crushed

1 tblspn chilli powder or to taste

750g (1½lb) tomatoes, peeled and chopped

1 tblspn chopped fresh oregano

Tabasco sauce, optional

60g (2oz) mature Cheddar cheese, grated

1 Rinse and drain kidney beans; place in a saucepan with water to cover. Bring to boil, boil hard for 10 minutes, then lower heat and simmer for an hour or until beans are tender. Drain thoroughly.

2 Heat oil in a saucepan, add onions, pepper and garlic and fry over gentle heat until tender. Stir in chilli powder and cook for 1 minute, then add tomatoes and oregano. Simmer, uncovered, for 30 minutes or until mixture thickens. Taste and add a dash or two of Tabasco if a hotter flavour is required.

3 Stir in beans and cheese and cook for 10 minutes more. Serve with rice or baked potatoes.

Serves 4

Poached Egg with Vinaigrette

4 eggs

1 lettuce

2 rindless streaky bacon rashers, fried or grilled until crisp

4 tblspn red wine vinegar

2 tblspn olive oil

¼ tspn crushed black peppercorns

2 tblspn red wine

1 Bring a large frying pan of water to the boil. Lower heat to a simmer. Break eggs into separate saucers. Using a draining spoon, swirl water, then slip in eggs, one at a time. Poach eggs until whites are set.

2 Arrange a bed of lettuce on four small plates. Top each portion with a poached egg and sprinkle with bacon.

3 Whisk vinegar, oil, pepper and red wine together in a small bowl. Pour a little of dressing over each portion and serve at once, with a garnish of extra crumbled bacon, if liked.

Serves 4

Penne with Caramelized Onion Sauce

45g (1½oz) butter

3 tblspn olive oil

1.5kg (3lb) onions, thinly sliced

1 tspn soft brown sugar

3 tblspn white wine vinegar

125ml (4fl oz) dry white wine

250ml (8fl oz) chicken stock

250ml (8fl oz) water

125g (4oz) Gruyère cheese, grated

500g (1lb) penne or other pasta shapes

3 tblspn finely chopped fresh parsley

1 Melt butter in oil in a heavy-based saucepan. Add onions. Cover pan and cook over low heat for about 40 minutes or until onions are tender. Stir occasionally.

2 Add sugar and vinegar to onions, increase heat and sauté, uncovered, for about 15 minutes or until onions are golden brown.

3 Add wine, stock and water. Bring to boil, then simmer for 5 minutes. Add Gruyère, whisking until melted.

4 Meanwhile, bring a large saucepan of lightly salted water to the boil. Add pasta and cook until just tender. Drain, tip into a heated bowl and add onion mixture. Toss well to combine, then sprinkle with the parsley and serve at once.

Serves 4-6

Potato Patties with Smoked Trout

3 potatoes, peeled and grated

1 large onion, grated

2 eggs, lightly beaten

2 tblspn plain flour

½ tspn crushed black peppercorns

30g (1oz) butter

8 slices smoked trout

60ml (2fl oz) soured cream

watercress and lemon slices for garnish

1 Put potatoes and onion in a clean tea-towel and squeeze out excess water. Tip into a bowl and add eggs, flour and pepper; mix to a batter.

2 Melt half the butter in a large frying pan. Add batter, 1-2 tablespoons at a time, to pan, leaving 2cm (¾in) between each patty. Cook patties for about 5 minutes on each side, or until golden. Drain on paper towels and keep hot. Cook rest of batter in the same way, adding more butter as required.

3 Arrange trout on serving plates, add two patties to each and garnish with soured cream, watercress and lemon slices.

Serves 4

Poached Egg with Vinaigrette, Potato Patties with Smoked Trout

MARVELLOUS MID-WEEK MEALS

It's great to come home to the mouthwatering aroma of a slow-cooked casserole or curry. This chapter also includes vegetarian dishes, a tasty meatloaf and a polenta pizza that is bound to become a family favourite.

Osso Buco

Osso Buco

1 tblspn olive oil
4 veal knuckles or veal shank slices, about 2cm (3/4in) thick
2 onions, finely chopped
2 carrots, finely chopped
2 sticks celery, finely chopped
2 cloves garlic, crushed
2 tblspn chopped fresh parsley
125ml (4fl oz) dry white wine
1 x 397g (13oz) can chopped tomatoes
1 x 60g (2oz) can tomato purée
250ml (8fl oz) chicken or veal stock

Gremolata

1 clove garlic, crushed
2 tblspn chopped fresh parsley
1 tspn grated lemon rind

1 Heat oil in a flameproof casserole. Add veal and brown on all sides. Remove veal and set aside. Add vegetables, garlic and parsley, cook, stirring, for 5 minutes.

2 Add wine, stirring to lift any sediment from base, stir in tomatoes, tomato purée and stock. Bring to the boil.

3 Return veal to casserole. Cover and simmer for 1 1/2-2 hours or until veal is tender.

4 Mix gremolata ingredients together, sprinkle over veal and cook for 2 minutes. Serve.

Serves 4

Lamb Curry

2 tblspn sunflower oil
1kg (2lb) lean leg lamb, cubed
3 onions, finely chopped
2 red chillies, seeded and finely chopped
2 cloves garlic, crushed
8 green cardamom pods, split
1 cinnamon stick
2 tblspn ground coriander
2 tblspn ground cumin
1 tspn turmeric
1 tspn grated nutmeg
2 tblspn freshly squeezed lime juice
1 tblspn paprika
300ml (10fl oz) natural low fat yogurt
1 tspn cornflour
1 x 397g (13oz) can chopped tomatoes
freshly ground black pepper

1 Heat oil in a saucepan. Brown lamb on all sides and set aside.

2 Add onions, chillies, garlic, cardamom and cinnamon. Cook for 10 minutes or until onions are golden and soft. Remove cinnamon stick and set it aside.

3 Stir in coriander, cumin, turmeric and nutmeg. Cook for 3-4 minutes or until spice mixture is dry; stir in lime juice and cook for 1 minute. Add paprika. Mix yogurt with cornflour; gradually stir into pan, then add tomatoes, and pepper.

4 Return lamb and cinnamon stick to pan and mix well. Cover and simmer for 1-1 1/2 hours, until tender. Remove cinnamon stick and serve.

Serves 6-8

Beef Braised in Beer

2 tblspn sunflower oil

1kg (2lb) topside beef, cut into chunks

2 large onions, cut into chunks

2 large carrots, cut into 1cm (1/2in) thick rounds

2 tblspn plain flour

125ml (4fl oz) beer

500ml (16fl oz) beef stock

2 cloves garlic, crushed

1 tblspn grated fresh root ginger

2 tblspn golden syrup

1 1/2 tblspn grated orange rind

1 Preheat oven to 180°C (350°F/ Gas 4). Heat the oil in a large nonstick frying pan over high heat. Add the beef cubes and sear until browned on all sides; using a slotted spoon transfer the cubes to a large ovenproof casserole.

2 Add onions and carrots to pan. Cook, stirring occasionally, for 5 minutes. Stir in flour and cook for 1 minute. Add beer with 125ml (4fl oz) of the stock. Stirring to lift up any browned bits on base of pan.

3 Stir in the remaining stock, garlic, ginger, golden syrup and orange rind. Stir into casserole, cover and braise for 1 3/4 hours or until tender.

Serves 4-6

Chicken Normandy

6 chicken breast fillets

2 tblspn olive oil

1 onion, sliced

2 Granny Smith apples, unpeeled, cored and sliced

375ml (12fl oz) unsweetened apple juice

2 tblspn honey

1 tblspn calvados or brandy

1 tblspn butter

salt

1 Preheat oven to 180°C (350°F/ Gas 4). Arrange the chicken fillets in a baking dish large enough to hold them in a single layer.

2 Heat the olive oil in a frying pan. Add the onion and sauté for about 5 minutes or until golden. Stir in the apples and sauté for 2-3 minutes more. Spoon the onion and apple mixture over the chicken.

3 Combine the apple juice and honey in a saucepan. Bring to the boil, stir in the calvados or brandy and remove the pan from the heat. Whisk in the butter and add salt to taste. Pour the sauce over the chicken.

4 Bake for 30-45 minutes, until the chicken is cooked through. Serve at once.

Serves 6

Beef Braised in Beer

Frankfurter and Bean Cobbler

Frankfurter and Bean Cobbler

2 tblspn sunflower oil

1 large onion, chopped

2 cloves garlic, crushed

185g (6oz) rindless streaky bacon, chopped

250g (8oz) button mushrooms, sliced

2 sticks celery, sliced

1 x 397g (13oz) can chopped tomatoes with herbs

1 tblspn cornflour

60ml (2fl oz) white wine

1 tblspn Worcestershire sauce

8 frankfurters, cut diagonally into 2cm (³/4in) chunks

375g (12oz) drained canned butterbeans

250g (8oz) self-raising flour

2 tblspn chopped fresh parsley

45g (1¹/2oz) butter

about 60ml (2fl oz) milk

milk to glaze

1 Preheat oven to 180°C (350°F/ Gas 4). Heat oil in a large flameproof casserole over moderate heat. Add onion, garlic and bacon and fry for 2 minutes. Stir in mushrooms and celery; fry for 2 minutes more. Stir in tomatoes.

2 Mix cornflour with white wine in a cup. Stir mixture into casserole and add Worcestershire sauce, frankfurters and butterbeans. Simmer mixture for 20 minutes.

3 Meanwhile, make topping. Combine flour and parsley in a mixing bowl. Rub in butter until mixture resembles fine breadcrumbs, then stir in enough milk to bind to a soft dough. Pat out dough on a floured surface and cut out rounds, using a 4cm (1¹/2in) scone cutter.

4 Arrange scones on top of mixture in casserole, brush tops with milk and bake for 35 minutes or until golden. Serve.

Serves 4

Kitchen Tip

If you do not have a scone cutter, use a large tumbler, dipping the rim in flour to prevent the scone dough from sticking to it.

Corn and Courgette Casserole

Corn and Courgette Casserole

2 tblspn mild olive oil

1 large onion, chopped

1 red pepper, chopped

5 courgettes, sliced

500g (1lb) drained canned or thawed frozen sweetcorn

3 ripe tomatoes, chopped

125ml (4fl oz) passata or puréed tomatoes

1 litre (1³/₄pt) vegetable stock

1 Heat oil in a large, deep frying pan. Add onion and red pepper and fry for 5 minutes over moderate heat, stirring occasionally. Add courgettes, sweetcorn, tomatoes and passata. Simmer for 15 minutes.

2 Add stock, bring to boil, then lower heat and simmer mixture for 25 minutes. Serve hot.

Serves 6

Polenta Pizza

Unlike yeast-based pizza dough, which needs time to rise, polenta dough can be baked as soon as it is made.

2 tblspn sunflower oil

280g (9oz) lean minced beef

1 small onion, finely chopped

2 cloves garlic, crushed

250ml (8fl oz) passata or puréed tomatoes

2 tblspn chopped fresh basil

½ tspn freshly ground black pepper

125g (4oz) polenta (corn meal)

125g (4oz) self-raising flour

1 tspn baking powder

155ml (5fl oz) milk

125g (4oz) Cheddar cheese, grated

1 red pepper, cut into thin strips

12 black olives

2 tblspn finely chopped fresh parsley

1 Preheat oven to 180°C (350°F/ Gas 4). Heat oil in a frying pan and fry minced beef until browned, stirring frequently. Using a slotted spoon, transfer mince to a bowl. Fry onion and garlic in fat remaining in pan. Stir in mince, passata, basil and pepper. Cook for 10 minutes, stirring.

2 Make the pizza base. Combine the polenta, flour and baking powder in a large bowl. Make a well in the centre, add the milk and mix to a dough. Knead lightly and roll out to fit a greased 28cm (11in) pizza pan or pie plate, pinching up the edges to form a rim.

3 Spread the mince mixture over the pizza base. Sprinkle with half the cheese and arrange the pepper strips on top. Dot with olives and sprinkle with the remaining cheese. Bake for 30 minutes, sprinkle with parsley and serve.

Serves 4-6

Polenta Pizza

Meatballs with Egg and Lemon Sauce

30g (1oz) butter

1 onion, chopped

90g (3oz) fresh white breadcrumbs

500g (1lb) minced beef or pork

30ml (1fl oz) red wine

4 eggs

plain flour for coating meatballs

600ml (1pt) chicken stock

2 tblspn water

3 tblspn lemon juice

cooked rice, to serve

1 Preheat oven to 150°C (300°F/ Gas 2). Melt butter in a frying pan, add onion and cook for 3 minutes. Tip into a bowl and add breadcrumbs, meat and wine. Lightly beat one egg and stir in to mixture. Mix to combine.

2 Take a rounded tablespoon of mixture and roll it to a ball between floured hands. Repeat with remaining mixture. Set meatballs aside.

3 Pour stock into a wide deep frying pan or saucepan and bring to boil. Carefully add the meatballs. When stock boils again, lower heat and simmer meatballs for 30 minutes, turning them occasionally. Using a slotted spoon, transfer meatballs to a baking dish and keep warm in oven.

4 Make sauce. Beat remaining eggs, water and lemon juice in a bowl. Stir in 3 tablespoons of hot stock, then add contents of bowl to pan. Stir sauce until it thickens but do not let it boil.

5 Serve meatballs on a bed of rice, with lemon sauce poured over top.

Serves 4

Greek Courgette Bake

125g (4oz) butter

1kg (2lb) courgettes, thickly sliced

2 tomatoes, peeled and chopped

2 tblspn chopped fresh dill

salt

freshly ground black pepper

6 eggs, beaten

45g (1½oz) Cheddar cheese, grated

1 Melt butter in a frying pan. Add courgettes, tomatoes and dill, stirring gently to coat the vegetables in melted butter. Season to taste, cover and cook for 30 minutes over gentle heat.

2 Pour eggs over vegetables. Sprinkle with cheese and cook for 3-4 minutes until cheese has melted and eggs have set.

Serves 4

Bean Hot Pot

315g (10oz) haricot beans, soaked overnight in water to cover

2 tblspn oil

2 onions, finely chopped

1 green pepper, chopped

500g (1lb) tomatoes, chopped

125ml (4fl oz) water

1 tblspn chopped fresh oregano

2 tspn mild chilli sauce

125g (4oz) Cheddar cheese, grated

1 Preheat oven to 180°C (350°F/ Gas 4). Drain beans, put them in a saucepan with water to cover and bring to boil. Boil vigorously for 10 minutes, then simmer for 1 hour or until tender. Drain.

2 Heat oil in a saucepan, add onions and pepper and stir fry until tender. Stir in tomatoes, water, oregano and chilli sauce. Bring to the boil, then simmer until thickened. Stir in beans.

3 Spoon mixture into an oven-proof dish, sprinkle with the cheese and bake for 20 minutes.

Serves 4

Bean Hot Pot

Curried Lamb Soup with Split Peas

Hearty Potato Soup

125g (4oz) smoked bacon, preferably in the piece, cut into 1cm (¹/₂in) cubes

185g (6oz) cabbage, shredded

4 potatoes, peeled and cut into 1cm (¹/₂in) cubes

1 large onion, roughly chopped

2 litres (3¹/₂pt) chicken stock

salt

freshly ground black pepper

allspice

3 tblspn chopped fresh parsley

1 Heat bacon in a heavy saucepan until the fat runs. Shake pan and continue to cook bacon until crisp. Add cabbage, lower heat, cover and cook for 10 minutes.

2 Add potatoes, onion and stock to pan, with salt, pepper and all-spice to taste. Bring to boil, lower heat and simmer for 30 minutes.

3 Remove the lid and cook for 15 minutes more, stirring. Serve sprinkled with the parsley.

Serves 6

Curried Lamb Soup with Split Peas

2 tblspn oil

410g (13oz) meaty lamb bones, such as shanks or shoulder

3 cloves garlic, crushed

1 onion, finely chopped

2 tblspn mild curry powder

185g (6oz) yellow split peas, soaked overnight in water to cover

1.2 litres (2pt) boiling water

2 tblspn chopped fresh mint

2 carrots, finely diced

2 sticks celery, sliced

60g (2oz) coconut cream

1 tblspn lemon juice

salt

snipped chives for garnish

1 Heat oil in a large saucepan over moderate heat. Add lamb bones and brown on all sides. Add garlic, onion and curry powder to pan and cook, stirring constantly, for 5 minutes. Drain peas and add them with boiling water.

2 Bring liquid to boil, skim off any surface scum, then lower heat. Simmer for 1 hour.

3 Remove lamb, slicing any meat remaining on bones into small pieces. Set aside. Purée soup in a blender or food processor, return to clean pan and add mint and carrots with sliced lamb. Bring to boil and cook until carrots are tender.

4 Stir in celery, coconut cream and lemon juice, with salt to taste. Serve in heated bowls, garnished with chives.

Serves 4-6

Chilli Beef Baked in Cornbread

1 tblspn olive oil

500g (1lb) lean minced beef

1 onion, chopped

1 red pepper, chopped

1 green pepper, chopped

1 clove garlic, crushed

2 tspn sambal oelek or Tabasco to taste

1 tblspn caster sugar

1 x 397g (13oz) can chopped tomatoes

2 tblspn red wine vinegar

60ml (2fl oz) red wine

1 tblspn tomato purée

185g (6oz) self raising flour

185g (6oz) polenta (corn meal)

2 tblspn sugar

250ml (8fl oz) milk

2 egg whites

2 tblspn corn oil

1 Preheat oven to 180°C (350°F/ Gas 4). Heat olive oil in a large nonstick frying pan. Add the beef, onion, red and green peppers, garlic, sambal oelek (if using) and sugar; cook for 5 minutes, stirring. Stir in the tomatoes, vinegar, wine and tomato purée. Simmer the mixture for about 10 minutes or until almost all the liquid has evaporated. If using Tabasco, stir it in now. Set the pan aside.

2 Make the cornbread. Combine the flour, polenta and sugar in a large bowl. Make a well in the centre. Whisk the milk, egg whites and oil together in a second bowl, pour the mixture into the well in the dry ingredients and mix swiftly; do not overmix.

3 Lightly grease an ovenproof baking dish and pour in the cornbread batter. Spoon the beef mixture into the centre of the batter, leaving a 4cm (1½in) border all round. Bake for 30 minutes. Serve hot.

Serves 4

Bacon-wrapped Meatloaf

This meatloaf is quite dense, making it an ideal candidate for slicing thinly for picnics and sandwiches.

45g (1½oz) All Bran breakfast cereal

15g (½oz) butter

500g (1lb) lean minced beef

375g (12oz) lean minced pork

4 spring onions, chopped

2 tblspn tomato purée

1 egg, lightly beaten

pinch dried thyme

1 tblspn chopped fresh parsley

250g (8oz) rindless streaky bacon rashers

1 Preheat oven to 180°C (350°F/ Gas 4). Process the bran cereal in a food processor until it has the texture of coarse crumbs.

2 Melt the butter in a heavy-based frying pan over moderate heat. Stir in the bran and cook, stirring constantly, for 2 minutes.

3 Transfer the bran to a large mixing bowl. Add the minced beef and pork, spring onions, tomato purée, egg, thyme and parsley. Mix thoroughly.

4 Line a 1kg (2lb) loaf tin with the bacon. Spoon the meat mixture into the tin, pressing it down lightly. Level the surface.

5 Bake the loaf for 1½ hours or until cooked through. Turn out onto a heated platter and serve with a selection of vegetables and a rich gravy or home-made tomato sauce. Alternatively, serve cold with chutney and salads.

Serves 6-8

Bacon-wrapped Meatloaf

Nobody should have to slave over a hot stove in summer, so give the cook a day off and enjoy a selection of simply delicious salads

Rare Beef Salad

2 tblspn olive oil

750g (1¹/₂lb) slice of best quality topside beef, about 5cm (2in) thick, trimmed

125g (4oz) button mushrooms, finely sliced

¹/₂ red pepper, chopped

2 tblspn chopped fresh parsley

60ml (2fl oz) olive oil

2 tpsn lemon juice

1 tblspn tarragon vinegar

1 tspn soft brown sugar

1 tspn crushed black peppercorns

2 cloves garlic, crushed

1 tblspn double cream

1 Preheat oven to 180°C (350°F/ Gas 4). Heat the oil in a large frying pan. When hot, add the beef and sear on all sides. Transfer to a roasting tin and roast for 10-15 minutes; the meat should be browned on the outside and rare in the centre. Set aside to cool.

2 Slice the beef downwards to give thin wafers of meat. Combine the beef slices, mushrooms, chopped pepper and parsley in a large bowl.

3 Mix the olive oil, lemon juice, vinegar, sugar, pepper, garlic and cream in a bowl. Whisk lightly, pour over the salad and toss well. Serve at once.

Serves 4-6

Avocado, Grapefruit and Pawpaw Salad with Prawns

1 Iceberg lettuce, shredded

1 radicchio lettuce, shredded

1 large avocado, halved, stoned, peeled and cut into chunks

1 large grapefruit, peeled and segmented

1 pawpaw, halved, seeded, peeled and cut into chunks

24 peeled cooked prawns

Dressing

5 tblspn white wine vinegar

1 egg yolk, beaten

1 clove garlic, crushed

125ml (4fl oz) olive oil

1 tblspn snipped fresh chives

salt

1 Make the dressing by mixing the vinegar, egg yolk, garlic, oil and chives, with salt to taste, in a screwtop jar. Close tightly; shake until well combined.

2 Mix the lettuces in a large bowl. Add just enough dressing to moisten; toss until lightly coated. Pile in the centre of four plates.

3 Arrange the avocado, grapefruit, pawpaw and prawns on and around the lettuce. Drizzle with a little more dressing and serve the rest separately.

Serves 4

Rare Beef Salad

Crunchy Chicken Salad

Fried Potato Salad

2 tblspn sunflower oil

250g (8oz) new potatoes, halved

1 large orange-fleshed sweet potato, peeled and cut into 1cm (1/2in) cubes

2 sticks celery, sliced

4 spring onions, finely chopped

1/2 small red cabbage, finely shredded

Dill Dressing

125ml (4fl oz) French dressing

1 tblspn chopped fresh parsley

1 tblspn Dijon mustard

1 tblspn chopped fresh dill

1 Make dressing by mixing all the ingredients in a screwtop jar. Close tightly; shake well.

2 Heat oil in a large saucepan. Add new potatoes with sweet potato cubes. Fry, turning frequently, until lightly browned and just tender. Drain on paper towels.

3 Combine fried potatoes with celery and spring onions in a bowl. Add dressing and toss lightly. Spread out cabbage on a large platter, top with fried potato salad and serve.

Serves 4

Crunchy Chicken Salad

4 cooked chicken breast fillets, cut into strips

250ml (8fl oz) soured cream or crème fraîche

125ml (4fl oz) mayonnaise

4 sticks celery, cut into short lengths

4 spring onions, finely chopped

60g (2oz) pecan nuts, roughly chopped

1 Arrange chicken in a large bowl. Whisk soured cream or crème fraîche with mayonnaise in a bowl. Spoon mixture over chicken.

2 Add celery, spring onions and pecans to salad and toss well.

Cover and chill before serving, garnished with fresh herbs if liked.

Serves 4

Mushroom Salad

250g (8oz) small button mushrooms, trimmed

125ml (4fl oz) French Dressing

2 tblspn crème fraîche

1 clove garlic, crushed

2 tblspn chopped fresh parsley

1 tspn snipped fresh chives

1 Arrange mushrooms in a shallow bowl large enough to hold them all in a single layer.

2 Combine French dressing, crème fraîche, garlic, parsley and chives in a bowl. Whisk until well mixed. Pour dressing over the mushrooms, cover bowl and refrigerate for at least 12 hours before serving.

Serves 4

Garden Vegetable Pasta Salad

250g (8oz) macaroni

salt

1 tblspn olive oil

2 carrots, sliced diagonally into 5mm (1/4in) slices

125g (4oz) French beans, topped, tailed and sliced diagonally into 2.5cm (1in) pieces

90g (3oz) shelled fresh or frozen peas

60g (2oz) fresh or frozen sweetcorn

30g (1oz) grated Parmesan cheese

Dressing

60ml (2fl oz) olive oil

2 tblspn red wine vinegar

3 tblspn chopped fresh parsley

1 tblspn chopped fresh basil

freshly ground black pepper

1 Make the dressing by mixing all the ingredients in a screwtop jar. Close tightly; shake until well combined.

2 Cook macaroni in a saucepan of lightly salted boiling water until just tender. Drain, rinse under cold water; drain again. Place in a salad bowl, add oil and toss.

3 Bring a small saucepan of water to the boil. Cook carrot slices for 3 minutes, remove with a slotted spoon, refresh under cold water and drain. Repeat the process with beans, cooking them for only 1 minute.

4 Add peas and corn to the boiling water and cook them until just tender. Drain, refresh under cold water and drain again.

5 Add beans, carrots, peas and corn to pasta, pour over dressing and toss to coat. Sprinkle salad with Parmesan and serve at once.

Serves 4

Salad Nicoise

200g (6½oz) green beans, topped and tailed

1 soft round lettuce, separated into leaves

1 radicchio lettuce, separated into leaves

1 x 200g (6½oz) can tuna in oil, drained and flaked

125g (4oz) cherry tomatoes, halved

90g (3oz) black olives

4 hard-boiled eggs, cut into quarters

6 drained canned anchovy fillets

Dressing

1 clove garlic, crushed

1/4 tspn freshly ground black pepper

1/2 tspn Dijon mustard

1 tblspn lemon juice

3 tblspn olive oil

1 Bring a saucepan of water to the boil, add beans and cook for 2 minutes. Drain, refresh under cold water and drain again.

2 Mix lettuce leaves in a salad bowl. Make dressing by mixing garlic, pepper, mustard, lemon juice and oil in a screwtop jar. Close tightly; shake until well combined. Add a little of dressing to mixed leaves and toss to coat.

3 Arrange tomatoes, beans, tuna, black olives, sliced eggs and anchovies on salad. Drizzle remaining dressing over top. Serve at once.

Serves 4-6

Salad Nicoise

Gruyère and Green Bean Salad

500g (1lb) green beans, topped and tailed

200g (6¹/₂oz) mushrooms, sliced

155g (5oz) Gruyère cheese, grated

60ml (2fl oz) olive oil

2 tblspn tarragon vinegar

1 tblspn Dijon mustard

¹/₄ tspn crushed black peppercorns

1 Bring a saucepan of water to the boil, add beans and cook for 1 minute. Drain, refresh under cold water and drain again. Place in a large salad bowl. Add mushrooms and cheese to bowl and mix lightly.

2 Make dressing by mixing oil, vinegar, mustard and pepper in a screwtop jar. Close tightly; shake until well combined. Pour dressing over salad and toss lightly.

Serves 4

Watercress Salad with Croûtons

1 bunch watercress, broken into sprigs

30g (1oz) pinenuts, toasted

45g (1¹/₂oz) butter

6 slices bread, crusts removed, cut into 1cm (¹/₂in) squares

4 rindless streaky bacon rashers

60ml (2fl oz) red wine vinegar

60ml (2fl oz) olive oil

1 tspn soft brown sugar

3 tblspn double cream

1 Arrange the watercress and pinenuts in a salad bowl.

2 Melt butter in a frying pan over moderate heat. Add bread and fry until golden. Remove with a slotted spoon and drain on paper towels. Fry bacon in fat remaining in pan; drain on paper towels, then crumble.

3 Sprinkle croûtons and bacon over salad. Whisk vinegar, oil, sugar and cream in a bowl, pour over salad and toss lightly. Serve.

Serves 4

Cottage Cheese and Fruit Salad

410g (13oz) cottage cheese

¹/₂ tspn grated orange rind

1 orange, segmented

30g (1oz) pecan nuts, halved and toasted

1 mignonette lettuce, separated into leaves

1 stick celery, sliced

1 red-skinned eating apple, thinly sliced

Orange Dressing

4 tblspn olive oil

2 tblspn freshly squeezed orange juice

1 tblspn red wine vinegar

¹/₂ tspn caster sugar

1 tspn each chopped fresh basil and tarragon

1 Make orange dressing by mixing all ingredients in a screwtop jar. Close tightly; shake until well combined.

2 Combine cottage cheese, orange rind and half the orange segments in a bowl. Add pecan nuts and mix lightly.

3 Divide lettuce between serving plates. Top with cottage cheese mixture. Arrange remaining orange, celery and apple around salads. Drizzle with dressing.

Serves 4

Crunchy Potato Salad

5 large potatoes, peeled and cubed

125g (4oz) cocktail onions, drained

8 hard-boiled eggs, quartered

2 tblspn drained capers

60g (2oz) roasted peanuts

125ml (4fl oz) olive oil

salt

freshly ground black pepper

Cook potatoes in a saucepan of lightly salted boiling water until just tender. Drain and cool to room temperature. Place in a salad bowl with onions, eggs, capers and peanuts. Drizzle olive oil over salad, season to taste and toss.

Serves 4

Pepper and Mushroom Salad

2 red peppers

2 green peppers

250g (8oz) button mushrooms, sliced

2 cloves garlic, crushed

2 tblspn red wine vinegar

1 tblspn olive oil

1 tspn crushed black peppercorns

1 Steam peppers over boiling water for 5 minutes. Cool slightly; cut into fine strips.

2 Mix peppers and mushrooms in a bowl. Whisk garlic, vinegar, oil and crushed peppercorns together in a small bowl. Pour the dressing over the salad and toss well.

Serves 4

Fennel Salad

1 large fennel bulb

60ml (2fl oz) lemon juice

5 tblspn olive oil

1 tspn freshly ground black pepper

pared rind of 1 orange, pith removed, cut into matchstick strips

60g (2oz) piece of Parmesan cheese

1 Cut leafy fronds from top of the fennel; set aside about 4 tablespoons. Cut bulb into thin slices. Place in a salad bowl.

2 Whisk lemon juice, olive oil and half the pepper together. Add dressing to fennel and toss.

3 Add fennel fronds and orange rind to salad and toss. Divide mixture between serving plates.

4 Using a cheese slicer or potato peeler, pare Parmesan cheese into paper-thin slices. Arrange slices over fennel, sprinkle with remaining black pepper and serve.

Serves 4

Crunchy Potato Salad, Pepper and Mushroom Salad

VEGETABLE VARIETY

Vegetables are usually viewed as accompaniments, but they can easily assume a starring role, as these delicious and unusual combinations prove. Dishes like Broccoli with Red Pepper Purée, Honey-glazed Carrot Straws and Turnips Dauphinoise are guaranteed to add glamour to any family meal.

Peas and Lettuce with Mint and Lemon

315g (10oz) frozen peas, thawed

15g (1/2oz) butter

2 tspn lemon juice

rind of 1/4 lemon, cut in fine matchstick strips

1 tblspn finely chopped fresh mint

1 head curly endive, torn into pieces

4 lemon slices for garnish

1 Cook peas in a saucepan of boiling water until just tender; drain well. Add butter and toss until coated.

2 Stir in lemon juice, lemon rind and mint.

3 Arrange peas with endive on individual plates, garnish with lemon slices and serve.

Serves 4

Honey-glazed Carrot Straws

1 tblspn corn oil

1 1/2 tblspn honey

2 tblspn red wine vinegar

6 carrots, cut into thin batons

watercress sprig for garnish

1 Heat the oil, honey and red wine vinegar in a medium frying pan over moderate heat for about 3 minutes or until the honey turns dark brown.

2 Add the carrots to the pan and toss in the honey glaze. Cook, stirring constantly, for 3 minutes or until tender.

3 Serve immediately, garnished with watercress.

Serves 4

Beans in Curry Cream

60g (2oz) butter

60g (2oz) flaked almonds

1 tblspn mild curry powder

1 red onion, chopped

500g (1lb) green beans, topped, tailed and halved

185ml (6fl oz) soured cream

1 Melt half the butter in a frying pan over moderate heat. Add almonds and curry powder and cook for 4 minutes, stirring constantly.

2 Transfer almond mixture to a serving dish; keep hot. Melt the remaining butter in pan, add onion and beans and cook for 3 minutes, stirring constantly.

3 Transfer onion and beans to the serving dish. Add cream to pan, bring to boil, then lower heat and simmer for 3 minutes or until slightly thickened.

4 Add sauce to vegetable mixture, toss well and serve.

Serves 4

Honey-glazed Carrot Straws, Peas and Lettuce with Mint and Lemon

Broccoli with Red Pepper Purée

500g (1lb) broccoli, cut into florets

1 tblspn olive oil

1 clove garlic, crushed

2 red peppers, chopped

125ml (4fl oz) chicken or vegetable stock

1 tblspn white wine vinegar

1 tspn chopped fresh tarragon

1 tspn horseradish cream

1 Boil, steam or microwave the broccoli until crisp-tender; tip into a serving dish and keep warm.

2 Heat the oil in a frying pan, add garlic and peppers and fry for 3-4 minutes until softened. Stir in remaining ingredients, bring to boil, then lower heat and simmer until pepper is tender. Purée red pepper mixture and spoon over broccoli.

Serves 4

Broccoli with Red Pepper Purée

Brussels Sprouts with Mustard Sauce

500g (1lb) brussels sprouts, trimmed

15g (½oz) butter

1 tblspn plain flour

125ml (4fl oz) hot milk

250ml (8fl oz) chicken or vegetable stock

2 tspn whole grain mustard

1 tblspn mayonnaise

1 Bring a saucepan of lightly salted water to the boil, add the sprouts; cook until crisp-tender.

2 Melt butter in a saucepan over moderate heat. Stir in flour. Cook for 1 minute, then gradually add milk and stock, stirring until mixture boils and thickens. Stir in mustard and mayonnaise.

3 Drain sprouts, tip into a heated bowl and pour over sauce.

Serves 4

Brussels Sprouts with Mustard Sauce

Leeks au Gratin

6 leeks

1 litre (1³/₄pt) chicken or vegetable stock

90g (3oz) Parmesan cheese in the piece

45g (1¹/₂oz) fresh white breadcrumbs

60g (2oz) butter, melted

1 Preheat oven to 180°C (350°F/ Gas 4). Remove leek tops and discard outer two layers of leaves. Trim bases, cut leeks in half lengthwise; rinse well and drain on paper towels.

2 Pour stock into a saucepan and bring to boil. Add leeks and cook for 4-5 minutes, then transfer to an ovenproof dish.

3 Grate cheese. Stir in breadcrumbs and butter, sprinkle over leeks and bake for 10-15 minutes.

Serves 6

Leeks au Gratin

Poached Baby Beetroot

1 bunch of baby beetroot, with stems

salt

125ml (4fl oz) soured cream

125ml (4fl oz) single cream

¹/₂ tspn cornflour

1 tblspn dry white wine

1 tblspn chopped fresh dill, plus dill sprig for garnish

1 Wash beetroot and twist off the leaves, leaving a little tuft of stem. Bring a large saucepan of lightly salted water to boil, add the beetroot and cook until just tender, about 20 minutes.

2 Drain beetroot, refresh under cold water and drain again. Remove peel, cut beetroot in half; drain on kitchen paper.

3 Combine soured cream, single cream, cornflour and wine in a saucepan. Slowly bring to boil, stirring constantly until sauce thickens slightly.

4 Stir in dill. Arrange beetroot in a serving dish, pour over sauce. Serve, garnished with dill sprig.

Serves 4

Poached Baby Beetroot

Courgette Gratin

2 tblspn olive oil
5 tblspn corn oil
1 kg (2lb) courgettes, thinly sliced
salt
freshly ground black pepper
1kg (2lb) tomatoes, thinly sliced
1 tblspn chopped fresh basil
185g (6oz) mozzarella cheese, thinly sliced

1 Preheat oven to 190°C (375°F/ Gas 5). Heat oils together in a large frying pan. Add courgettes and sauté lightly for about 5 minutes, turning frequently. Drain on paper towels.

2 Transfer courgettes to a baking dish and add salt and pepper to taste. Arrange tomato slices and chopped basil on top. Cover with mozzarella.

3 Bake for about 25 minutes, until mozzarella has melted and topping is golden. Serve hot.

Serves 6

Rosemary Potatoes

500g (1lb) potatoes, peeled and thinly sliced
60g (2oz) butter
1 clove garlic, crushed
1 tblspn finely chopped fresh rosemary

1 Bring a large saucepan of water to boil. Add potatoes. When water boils again, remove pan from heat and drain potatoes in a colander. Pat dry with paper towels.

2 Melt butter in a large frying pan over moderate heat. Add garlic, potato slices and rosemary.

3 Sauté potatoes until lightly golden and cooked through. Shake pan frequently to prevent them from sticking, and turn them over occasionally with a spatula. Serve at once, in a heated dish.

Serves 4

Broad Beans with Yogurt Dressing, Glazed Onions

Broad Beans with Yogurt Dressing

125ml (4fl oz) olive oil

750g (1½lb) shelled fresh or thawed frozen broad beans

2 tblspn snipped chives

60ml (2fl oz) lemon juice

2 tblspn chopped fresh dill

500ml (16fl oz) water

185ml (6fl oz) natural low fat yogurt

2 cloves garlic, crushed

1 Heat oil in a large saucepan over moderate heat. Add broad beans and chives and sauté for 3 minutes.

2 Add lemon juice, dill and measured water. Bring to boil, lower heat, cover and simmer for 10 minutes.

3 Drain broad beans and tip them into a serving dish. Cool to room temperature.

4 Combine yogurt and garlic in a bowl. Spoon mixture over broad beans. Add a fresh dill garnish if liked.

Serves 6

Turnips Dauphinoise

3 turnips

500ml (16fl oz) single cream

½ tspn crushed black peppercorns

1 tspn ground cumin

1 Preheat oven to 180°C (350°F/ Gas 4). Peel turnips and cut them into 1cm (½in) thick rounds. Cut each round into quarters and add to a saucepan of boiling water. Cook for 7 minutes, drain and place in a serving dish.

2 Bring cream, pepper and cumin to boil in a saucepan over high heat. Stir constantly until mixture has reduced by one third.

3 Pour sauce over turnips, cover dish and bake for 20 minutes. Serve at once.

Serves 4

Vegetables with Garlic and Lemon Juice

8 new potatoes, scrubbed and thinly sliced

salt

90g (3oz) frozen peas, thawed

3 tblspn olive oil

2 cloves garlic, crushed

1 leek, white part only, sliced

1 red pepper, cut into strips

125g (4oz) mangetout, trimmed

½ tspn crushed black peppercorns

2 tblspn lemon juice

1 Cook the potatoes in a large saucepan of lightly salted water until just tender. Using a slotted spoon, transfer the potatoes to a bowl and set aside.

2 Add the peas to the boiling water and cook for 3 minutes; drain, refresh under cold water, drain again and set aside.

3 Heat the oil in a large frying pan or wok. Add the garlic, leek, red pepper strips, mangetout, peas and potatoes. Stir fry for 2-3 minutes. Stir in the pepper and lemon juice, toss well and serve.

Serves 4

Glazed Onions

20 small white onions, halved lengthwise or 40 pickling onions, peeled but left whole

60g (2oz) butter

2 tblspn soft brown sugar

1 Bring a large saucepan of water to the boil, add onions and cook for 5 minutes. Drain well and pat dry on paper towels.

2 Heat butter in a large frying pan. Stir in sugar until dissolved. Add onions and cook for 5-10 minutes, shaking pan constantly to turn them over in glaze and prevent them from sticking. When onions are golden brown, transfer them to a heated dish and serve.

Serves 4-6

SUNDAY BEST

Sunday lunch is more than a meal – it's a tradition, a social occasion, a chance to catch up on all the goings on within the family. What better time to enjoy perfectly-cooked Leg of Lamb with Plum Sauce, or Old-fashioned Beef Pot Roast with Tomatoes? This chapter has something for all palates and pockets, from Roast Chicken with Orange Prune Stuffing to a perfect Steak and Kidney Pie.

Roast Sirloin with Herb Sauce

1.5kg (3lb) sirloin roast, preferably aged sirloin

freshly ground black pepper

2 tblspn Dijon mustard

Herb Sauce

30g (1oz) fresh flat-leaf parsley, leaves stripped from stalks

15g (1/2oz) fresh coriander, leaves stripped from stalks

6 dill sprigs

6 spring onions, roughly chopped

125ml (4fl oz) olive oil

yolk of 1 hard-boiled egg

1 large clove garlic, halved

2 tblspn lemon juice

1 tspn Dijon mustard

salt

freshly ground black pepper

1 Preheat oven to 160°C (325°F/ Gas 2). Season sirloin with freshly ground pepper; brush with mustard. Bake in a roasting tin for 1 1/2 hours or until a meat thermometer inserted in thickest part of the roast shows an internal temperature of 71°C (160°F).

2 Transfer meat to a board for carving, cover it loosely with a foil tent and set aside for 15 minutes. If preferred, allow meat to cool to room temperature.

3 Meanwhile make herb sauce. Combine all ingredients except seasoning in a blender or food processor; purée until smooth. Scrape into a bowl; season to taste.

4 Carve meat into thin slices. Serve with herb sauce.

Serves 6-8

Baked Lamb with Dried Pears

500g (1lb) dried pears

1kg (2lb) boned and rolled leg of lamb

60ml (2fl oz) sherry

60ml (2fl oz) white wine

1/2 tspn crushed black peppercorns

1 tblspn soft brown sugar

2 tblspn peach or apricot jam

2 green peppers, cut into 2cm (3/4in) squares

1 Preheat oven to 180°C (350°F/ Gas 4). Put pears in a bowl with water to cover; soak for 30 minutes.

2 Tie lamb into a neat shape with string, place it in a roasting tin and bake for 45 minutes. Drain off any excess fat.

3 Drain pears, pat them dry on kitchen paper and arrange around lamb in the roasting tin. Mix sherry, wine, pepper, sugar and jam in a small bowl; pour mixture over lamb and pears and bake for 45 minutes more.

4 Add peppers to tin and bake for 10-15 minutes, until just tender. Serve lamb surrounded by pears and peppers. Add a chopped parsley garnish if liked.

Serves 4-6

Roast Pork with Apricot Prune Stuffing

125g (4oz) dried apricots, chopped

4 spring onions, sliced

90g (3oz) pitted prunes, chopped

125g (4oz) macadamia nuts or almonds, chopped

2 tblspn mixed candied peel

45g (1 1/2oz) fresh breadcrumbs

1 tblspn chopped fresh basil

30g (1oz) butter, melted

1.5-2kg (3-4 1/2lb) loin of pork, boned

2 tblspn honey, melted

2 tblspn lemon juice

1 Preheat oven to 180°C (350°F/ Gas 4). Combine apricots, spring onions, prunes, nuts and mixed peel in a blender or food processor. Process for about 30 seconds or until roughly chopped. Scrape mixture into a large bowl. Stir in breadcrumbs, basil and butter; mix well.

2 Spread stuffing evenly over pork flesh. Carefully roll meat up and tie it securely with string. Put meat in a roasting tin and roast it for 1 1/2 hours or until cooked to taste.

3 Halfway through cooking time, mix honey and lemon juice in a cup; baste pork with mixture.

4 Transfer pork to a serving platter. Garnish with water-cress, if liked.

Serves 6-8

Baked Lamb with Dried Pears, Roast Pork with Apricot Prune Stuffing

Old-fashioned Beef Pot Roast with Tomatoes

Old-fashioned Beef Pot Roast with Tomatoes

45g (1¹/₂oz) butter

1.5-2kg (3-4¹/₂lb) beef topside, trimmed

1 onion, finely chopped

2 cloves garlic, crushed

4 carrots, sliced

185ml (6fl oz) beef stock

1 x 397g (13oz) can chopped tomatoes with herbs

125ml (4fl oz) dry white wine

125ml (4fl oz) passata or puréed tomatoes

¹/₂ tspn crushed black peppercorns

1 Melt butter in a large, deep flameproof casserole over moderate heat. Add beef and sear well on all sides. Remove meat from casserole and set aside.

2 Add onion, garlic and carrots to casserole and fry until golden. Return meat and add remaining ingredients. Bring to boil, cover and simmer for 1¹/₂ hours.

3 Turn meat and spoon cooking juices over top. Replace cover and cook for 45 minutes more. Transfer the meat to a serving dish, cover with foil and set aside.

4 Boil vegetables and cooking liquid for 5 minutes or until thickened. Carve pot roast into thick slices and serve, coated with sauce.

Serves 6-8

Rolled Veal with Wild Mushroom Stuffing

60g (2oz) dried wild mushrooms

90g (3oz) butter

1 red onion, very finely chopped

2 spring onions, very finely chopped

2 cloves garlic, crushed

1 tblspn soft brown sugar

1 tblspn snipped chives

1 tblspn chopped fresh parsley

45g (1¹/₂oz) fresh white breadcrumbs

2 tblspn French onion soup mix

2kg (4lb) loin of veal, boned

2 tblspn apricot jam

2 tblspn concentrated orange juice

Rolled Veal with Wild Mushroom Stuffing

1 Preheat oven to 180°C (350°F/ Gas 4). Soak mushrooms in water for 20 minutes; drain and chop.

2 Heat 30g (1oz) of butter in a frying pan, add onion, spring onions, garlic and sugar and cook for 2 minutes. Stir in mushrooms, chives, parsley, breadcrumbs and soup mix.

3 Open veal out and spread the stuffing over flesh. Roll veal tightly, tie with string and place in a roasting tin. Melt rest of butter in a small pan, stir in jam and orange juice and brush veal with mixture. Roast for 1¼ hours, basting several times with remaining orange mixture.

Serves 6-8

Leg of Lamb with Plum Sauce

1.5kg (3lb) leg of lamb
freshly ground black pepper
250ml (8fl oz) red wine
1 onion, chopped
16 plums, halved and stoned
¼ tspn allspice
1 tblspn red wine vinegar

1 Preheat oven to 180°C (350°F/ Gas 4). Put lamb in a roasting tin, season with pepper and baste with red wine. Roast for 1½-2 hours, opting for shorter time if you like your lamb 'pink'. Halfway through cooking time add onion and plums to tin. Baste occasionally.

2 When meat is cooked, transfer it to a hot dish and stand it under a foil tent for at least 15 minutes before carving.

3 Strain contents of roasting tin through a sieve into a large jug. Force solids through sieve into a saucepan. Skim fat from liquid in jug; stir liquid into pan. If necessary, boil sauce to reduce it. Add allspice and vinegar and pour into a sauceboat.

4 Carve the meat onto a platter and serve with the plum sauce.

Serves 6

Saddle of Lamb with Mustard

2 cloves garlic, crushed

2 tblspn Dijon mustard

2 tblspn whole grain mustard

2 tblspn tarragon vinegar

1 kg (2lb) saddle of lamb, trimmed and boned

30g (1oz) packaged dry breadcrumbs

1 Preheat oven to 180°C (350°F/ Gas 4). Mix garlic, mustards and vinegar in a small bowl. Brush mixture over lamb. Tie lamb into a neat shape with string, place in a roasting tin and roast for 20 minutes.

2 Sprinkle breadcrumbs over the surface of lamb, pressing them in slightly. Return lamb to oven and roast for 15 minutes more or until cooked to your taste. Serve with vegetables.

Serves 4

Steak and Kidney Pie

30g (1oz) plain flour

salt

freshly ground black pepper

1.5kg (3lb) chuck or blade steak, cut into bite-size pieces

250g (8oz) kidneys, skinned, cored and quartered

8 spring onions, chopped

60g (2oz) butter

300ml (10fl oz) beef stock

1 bay leaf

1 tblspn chopped fresh parsley

1 tblspn dry sherry

1 tspn Worcestershire sauce

1 x 215g (7oz) packet frozen puff pastry, thawed

beaten egg yolk to glaze

1 Put flour in a strong polythene bag with salt and pepper to season. Add steak and kidneys, close bag tightly and shake to coat. Tip contents of bag into a sieve; shake off excess flour.

Saddle of Lamb with Mustard

2 Sauté spring onions in butter in a large saucepan until transparent. Add steak and kidney in batches and brown on all sides, stirring constantly. Add stock, bay leaf and parsley, with salt and pepper to taste. Simmer, covered, for 1-1¼ hours or until meat is tender. Remove bay leaf. Stir in sherry and Worcestershire sauce; set aside to cool slightly.

3 Preheat oven to 220° (425°C/ Gas 7). Lightly butter a pie dish, place a funnel in centre. Spoon meat around funnel, then roll out pastry on a floured surface to fit dish. Slash small vents in pastry, decorate top with pastry leaves and glaze with egg yolk. Bake for 10 minutes, then lower heat to 190°C (375°F/Gas 5) and bake for 15-20 minutes more, until pastry is golden.

Serves 6

Pork and Pear Pie

750g (1½lb) lean pork, cut into 2cm (¾in) cubes

1 large onion, roughly chopped

2 cloves garlic, crushed

1 x 60g (2oz) can tomato purée

2 tblspn fruit chutney

300ml (10fl oz) chicken stock

5 tblspn dry white wine

3 pears, peeled, cored and thinly sliced

1 tspn crushed black peppercorns

1 x 215g (7oz) frozen puff pastry, thawed

milk to glaze

1 Combine pork, onion, garlic, tomato purée, chutney, stock and wine in a large saucepan. Bring to boil, lower heat and simmer, uncovered, for 1 hour. Stir occasionally. Transfer mixture to an ovenproof pie dish, arrange the pear slices on top and sprinkle with pepper.

2 Preheat oven to 190°C (375°F/ Gas 5). Roll out pastry on a floured surface and cover top of pie; pinch edges and decorate with trimmings, if liked. Glaze pastry with milk and bake pie for 35 minutes. Serve hot.

Serves 4

Caraway Chicken

3 tspn caraway seeds

60g (2oz) butter, softened

1 x 1.5kg (3lb) chicken

1½ tblspn plain flour

125ml (4fl oz) chicken stock

2 tblspn dry white wine

1 Preheat oven to 180°C (350°F/ Gas 4). Grind 2 teaspoons of caraway seeds. Beat butter until fluffy; stir in caraway seeds.

2 Carefully loosen skin from chicken breast to create a pocket. Spoon three quarters of caraway butter into space between chicken skin and breast meat, patting it out as evenly as posible. Melt remaining caraway butter in a small saucepan; reserve.

3 Sprinkle remaining caraway seeds inside chicken cavity. Place chicken breast-side up on a rack in a roasting tin. Brush with half reserved caraway butter.

4 Roast chicken for 30 minutes, brush with remaining caraway butter, then roast for 1½ hours, basting every 20 minutes.

5 Tip chicken so that any juices flow into roasting tin. Transfer chicken to a serving platter and keep warm. Pour pan juices into a measuring jug; skim about 2 tablespoons of fat off top and place in a frying pan. Discard any remaining fat. Make up pan juices to 250ml (8fl oz) with water.

6 Heat fat in pan and stir in flour. Cook for 1 minute, then gradually add pan juices, stock and wine, stirring until sauce boils and thickens. Simmer, stirring constantly, for 3 minutes. Season to taste.

7 Carve chicken and serve with the hot sauce.

Serves 4

Poussins with Wild Rice Stuffing

4 tblspn corn oil

45g (1½oz) fresh white breadcrumbs

1 clove garlic, crushed

90g (3oz) cooked wild rice

1 tblspn dried mixed herbs

90g (3oz) drained canned apricots, finely chopped

4 oven-ready poussins

30g (1oz) butter

4 tblspn apricot jam

1 tblspn honey

1 Preheat oven to 180°C (350°F/ Gas 4). Heat oil in a large frying pan. Add breadcrumbs and garlic and cook for 1 minute, stirring. Add rice herbs and apricots and mix well. Fill each poussin with stuffing.

2 Melt butter in a saucepan, add the jam and honey and stir until dissolved. Brush each poussin with apricot glaze. Bake in a roasting tin for 40 minutes, basting the poussins frequently with glaze.

Serves 4

Roast Chicken with Orange Prune Stuffing

250g (8oz) cooked long-grain rice

2 oranges, peeled, segmented and chopped

185g (6oz) pitted prunes, chopped

6 spring onions, sliced

1.5kg (3lb) chicken

60g (2oz) butter, melted

1 tspn dried oregano

1 tspn dried basil

1 tspn finely grated orange rind

Preheat oven to 180°C (350°F/Gas 4). Mix rice, oranges, prunes and spring onions. Stuff chicken with mixture, place in a greased roasting tin and brush with a mixture of butter, herbs and orange rind. Roast for 1¼ hours or until golden and cooked.

Serves 6

Soy-glazed Roast Duck

60ml (2fl oz) soy sauce

1 tblspn five spice powder

1 tblspn grated fresh root ginger

1 tblspn sherry

2.25kg (5lb) duck

1 Mix soy sauce, spice powder, ginger and sherry in a shallow dish. Add duck. Marinate for 3 hours, basting and turning frequently.

2 Preheat oven to 190°C (375°F/ Gas 5). Drain duck, reserving marinade, and prick it all over with a fork. Place on a rack in a roasting tin; roast for 30 minutes.

3 Pour away most of fat from tin. Pour marinade over duck. Roast for 1-1¼ hours more, basting frequently, until cooked.

Serves 4

Roast Chicken with Cheese Stuffing

155g (5oz) butter

2 tblspn chopped fresh herbs

125g (4oz) Parmesan cheese, grated

2 tblspn fruit chutney

125g (4oz) packaged dried breadcrumbs

1 egg, lightly beaten

1 x 1.5kg (3lb) chicken

2 cloves garlic, crushed

1 Preheat oven to 180°C (350°F/ Gas 4). Melt 90g (3oz) of butter in a saucepan. Stir in herbs, Parmesan, chutney and bread-crumbs, with enough of egg to bind. Stuff chicken with this mixture.

2 Melt remaining butter in clean pan; add garlic and brush mixture over chicken. Roast for 1¼-1½ hours or until cooked through, basting occasionally.

Serves 4

Roast Chicken with Cheese Stuffing

OLD-FASHIONED PUDDINGS

Don't call them desserts – these are puddings, plain and simple and absolutely irresistible. Lemon Delicious; Raspberry Fool; Rhubarb Crumble; Plum Clafouti; Bread and Butter Pudding with Dates: whatever the weather, they always go down well.

Baked Pears

45g (1oz) butter

3 tblspn soft brown sugar

3 large pears, halved and cored

185ml (6fl oz) double cream

1 Preheat oven to 200°C (400°F/ Gas 6). Grease a baking dish with a little of the butter. Sprinkle half the sugar on the bottom and sides of the dish.

2 Place the pears cut-side down in the dish, sprinkle with the remaining sugar and dot with the remaining butter.

3 Bake for 10 minutes. Pour the cream over the pears and bake for 25-30 minutes more. Serve warm.

Serves 6

Blackberry and Apple Brown Betty

500g (1lb) fresh blackberries, hulled

2 Bramley apples, peeled, cored and thinly sliced

90g (3oz) soft brown sugar

1/2 tspn ground cinnamon

grated rind and juice of 1/2 lemon

155g (5oz) fresh wholemeal breadcrumbs

60g (2oz) butter, melted

cream or crème fraîche to serve

1 Preheat oven to 180°C (350°F/ Gas 4). Mix the blackberries, apple slices, sugar, cinnamon, lemon rind and juice in a baking dish.

2 In a bowl, combine the breadcrumbs with the melted butter, stirring to coat the crumbs thoroughly. Spread over the fruit mixture.

3 Bake for 50 minutes or until the topping is golden brown. Serve warm, offering the cream or crème fraîche separately.

Serves 6

Plum Clafouti

butter for greasing

1 x 825g (1lb 10oz) can plums, drained and sliced, or 750g (1½lb) fresh plums, poached, drained and sliced

1 egg plus 3 egg yolks

125g (4oz) caster sugar

125ml (4fl oz) single cream

1 tblspn plain flour

2 tblspn lemon juice

1 Preheat oven to 180°C (350°F/ Gas 4). Butter a 23cm (9in) flan dish; arrange the plums on the base as evenly as possible.

2 Combine the whole egg and yolks with the sugar in a mixing bowl. Beat with a hand-held electric mixer until creamy. Add the cream, flour and lemon juice and mix well.

3 Pour the mixture over the plums, taking care not to disturb them. Bake for 30 minutes or until the top is golden. Serve dusted with sifted icing sugar if liked.

Serves 6

Plum Clafouti

Queen of Puddings

butter for greasing

300ml (10fl oz) milk

3 eggs, separated

1/4 tspn vanilla essence

220g (7oz) caster sugar

90g (3oz) fresh white breadcrumbs

3 tblspn raspberry jam

2 tblspn lemon juice

1 Preheat oven to 180°C (350°F/ Gas 4). Grease a baking dish with butter. Combine milk, egg yolks and vanilla essence with 30g (1oz) of sugar in a large jug; beat until well mixed. Put breadcrumbs in a bowl, pour over milk mixture and set aside for 15 minutes.

2 Spoon crumb mixture into baking dish and bake for 30 minutes; cool slightly. Combine jam and lemon juice. Spread mixture over pudding.

3 Beat egg whites until stiff peaks form. Gradually add remaining sugar, beating constantly until mixture is stiff and glossy. Spoon meringue over pudding and bake for 20 minutes.

Serves 6

Orange Rice Pudding

315g (10oz) pudding rice

250ml (8fl oz) single cream

375ml (12fl oz) water

2 tspn vanilla essence

1/2 tspn ground cinnamon

750ml (1 1/4pt) milk

2 egg yolks

125g (4oz) caster sugar

2 tblspn grated orange rind

90g (3oz) sultanas

185ml (6fl oz) freshly squeezed orange juice

1 Preheat oven to 180°C (350°F/ Gas 4). Combine rice, cream, measured water, vanilla and cinnamon in a large saucepan. Add half the milk. Stir over moderate heat for about 20 minutes, until rice has absorbed most of liquid.

2 Beat egg yolks, sugar and lemon rind in a large bowl until thick and creamy. Stir in rice mixture, sultanas, orange juice and remaining milk; mix well. Pour mixture into a soufflé dish and bake for 30 minutes.

Serves 6

Apple Meringue

1kg (2lb) Bramley apples, peeled and sliced

155ml (5fl oz) water

1 tblspn lemon juice

125g (4oz) sugar

Meringue

4 egg whites

125g (4oz) caster sugar

2 tblspn flaked almonds, toasted

1 Preheat oven to 180°C (350°F/ Gas 4). Combine sliced apples, measured water and lemon juice in a saucepan. Cook for 20 minutes or until apples are soft. Drain, return apples to clean pan, add sugar and beat to a smooth purée. Spoon into a 20cm (8in) soufflé dish.

2 Beat egg whites until thick. Add sugar, 1 tablespoon at a time, continuing to beat mixture until stiff peaks form. Fold in almonds.

3 Pile almond meringue on top of apple purée and bake for 30 minutes or until topping golden.

Serves 6

Lemon Delicious Pudding

60g (2oz) butter plus extra for greasing

90g (3oz) caster sugar

grated rind and juice of 1 large lemon

2 eggs, separated

30g (1oz) self-raising flour

185ml (6fl oz) milk

1 Preheat oven to 180°C (350°F/ Gas 4). Grease a 1 litre (1 3/4pt) soufflé dish. Cream butter with sugar and lemon rind until pale and fluffy. Stir in egg yolks, flour and lemon juice. Gradually stir in milk.

2 Whisk egg whites until stiff. Fold into lemon mixture, spoon mixture into prepared dish and place dish in a roasting tin half filled with boiling water. Bake for 45 minutes until sponge topping is golden.

Serves 4

Lemon Delicious Pudding

Bread and Butter Pudding with Dates

Raspberry Fool

500g (1lb) fresh or thawed frozen raspberries

60g (2oz) caster sugar

1 tspn lemon juice

300ml (10fl oz) whipping cream

1 Purée raspberries with sugar and lemon juice in a blender or food processor. Press purée through a sieve into a clean bowl to remove all seeds.

2 In a separate bowl, whip cream to soft peaks. Fold it into raspberry purée.

3 Spoon fool into a glass serving bowl or individual glass dishes. Cover and refrigerate for at least 1 hour before serving.

Serves 4-6

Baked Rice Pudding

30g (1oz) butter plus extra for greasing

600ml (1pt) milk

60g (2oz) pudding rice

2 tblspn caster sugar

pinch salt

1 tspn ground cinnamon

single cream to serve

1 Preheat oven to 160°C (325°F/ Gas 3). Butter a baking dish. Pour in milk, rice, sugar, salt and cinnamon. Stir well to combine.

2 Bake pudding for 15 minutes. Stir well, bake for 15 minutes more, then stir again.

3 Lower heat to 150°C (300°F/ Gas 2). Return pudding to oven and cook for 1¹/₂-2 hours more, or until topping is golden, most of milk has been absorbed and pudding is creamy. Serve warm, with cream.

Serves 4

Bread and Butter Pudding with Dates

60g (2oz) butter, softened

10 slices day-old sliced white bread, crusts removed

4 eggs

125g (4oz) caster sugar

2 tblspn finely grated lemon rind

300ml (10fl oz) double cream

300ml (10fl oz) milk

1 tspn ground cinnamon

155g (5oz) pitted dates, chopped

1 Preheat oven to 170°C (325°F/ Gas 3). Butter bread generously; cut it into 4cm (1¹/₂in) squares.

2 Beat eggs with sugar until thick. Stir in lemon rind, cream, milk and cinnamon. Add bread and dates, mix well and soak for 30 minutes. Pour mixture into a greased ovenproof dish and bake for 1-1¹/₄ hours.

Serves 8

Walnut Pudding

75g (2½oz) butter, plus extra for greasing

90g (3oz) soft brown sugar

1 egg

125g (4oz) self-raising flour

1 tspn ground ginger

¼ tspn grated nutmeg

½ tspn ground cinnamon

¼ tspn ground cloves

60ml (2fl oz) milk

45g (1½oz) walnuts, chopped

1 Preheat oven to 180°C (350°F/ Gas 4). Cream butter with sugar in a mixing bowl until light and fluffy. Beat in egg, then add flour and spices alternately with milk. Stir in walnuts and mix well.

2 Grease a pudding basin. Spoon walnut mixture into basin, cover with foil and place in a roasting tin half-filled with boiling water.

3 Bake for 1½-1¾ hours or until a skewer inserted in pudding comes out clean. Turn pudding out onto a heated plate and serve with custard and a fresh fruit decoration, if liked.

Baked Apples with Sabayon

4 Bramley apples

125g (4oz) mincemeat

crystallized orange peel, cut into diamond shapes, to decorate

Sabayon

2 eggs

2 tblspn grated orange rind

2 tblspn caster sugar

60ml (2fl oz) freshly squeezed orange juice

1 tblspn double cream

1 Make sabayon. Place eggs in a heatproof bowl. Add orange rind and caster sugar and whisk lightly. Place bowl over a saucepan of simmering water and continue to whisk for about 5 minutes or until eggs are so pale as to be almost white in colour.

2 Remove bowl from heat and gradually whisk in orange juice and then cream. Continue to whisk sabayon for 3 minutes more. Cover bowl, cool, then chill for 2 hours.

3 Preheat oven to 180°C (350°F/ Gas 4). Core apples but do not peel them. Slice a thin layer off the bottom of each apple so that they will stand straight. Score skin around the equator on each apple to prevent splitting.

4 Arrange apples in a baking dish. Spoon mincemeat into centre of each. Bake for 30-45 minutes until tender.

5 Serve apples with the sabayon, decorated with crystallized orange rind.

Serves 4

Variations
Instead of using mincemeat, try filling the apples with one of the following: pitted prunes with almonds; chopped ready-to-eat dried apricot mixed with apricot jam and a little lemon juice; chopped dates with glacé pineapple or sultanas with brown sugar.

Walnut Pudding

Baked Apples with Sabayon

Easy Blackcurrant Sponge

Rhubarb Gratin

45g (1½ oz) butter, cut into small pieces, plus extra for greasing

125g (4oz) granulated sugar

60g (2oz) soft brown sugar

1 tspn ground cinnamon

1kg (2lb) rhubarb, trimmed and cut into 2.5cm (1in) lengths

90ml (3fl oz) single cream

1 Preheat oven to 190°C (375°F/ Gas 5). Grease a baking dish. Mix granulated sugar, brown sugar and cinnamon in a small bowl.

2 Layer rhubarb in dish, sprinkling each layer with a little of sugar mixture and adding a few pieces of butter. Sprinkle the remaining sugar mixture over top and dot with rest of butter. Bake for 20 minutes.

3 Pour cream around rhubarb. Bake for 5 minutes more, or until cream bubbles and rhubarb starts to brown in places. Serve hot.

Serves 4

Easy Blackcurrant Sponge

3 tblspn Crème de Cassis

125g (4oz) caster sugar

2 tblspn lemon juice

185g (6oz) blackcurrant jam

60ml (2fl oz) water

1 x 20cm (8in) sponge cake

Coulis

375g (12oz) blackcurrants

60g (2oz) caster sugar

To Serve whipped cream, fresh blackcurrants and mint sprigs

1 Make the coulis. Combine the blackcurrants and sugar in a saucepan. Cook over low heat, stirring constantly, for 5 minutes, then press through a sieve into a bowl. Cool, then chill for at least 1 hour.

2 Combine the Crème de Cassis, caster sugar, lemon juice, blackcurrant jam and water in a medium saucepan. Heat gently, stirring, until sugar and jam have dissolved. Simmer for 5 minutes.

3 Put sponge cake on a heat-proof plate; spoon hot syrup over top. Set aside until cold.

4 To serve, place a slice of sponge on each dessert plate. Spoon a little of the coulis on the side and add a rosette of whipped cream. Decorate with fresh blackcurrants and mint.

Serves 6

Spicy Apple Charlotte

125g (4oz) apricot jam

125ml (4fl oz) water

1 tblspn lemon juice

1kg (2lb) Bramley apples, peeled and sliced

1 tspn ground mixed spice

2 tblspn sultanas

1 white sandwich loaf, thickly sliced

60g (2oz) butter, melted

1 Melt jam with measured water and lemon juice in a saucepan. Add apples. Cook gently until apples form a purée. Drain any excess liquid, transfer purée to a bowl and stir in spice and sultanas. Cool completely.

2 Preheat oven to 180°C (350°F/ Gas 4). Remove crusts from bread. Use a little of the butter to grease a charlotte mould or 16cm (6½in) loose-based cake tin. Line bottom of tin with bread, cutting it to fit snugly and dipping each slice or piece in butter before fitting it in place. Use more butter-dipped bread slices to line the sides.

3 Fill bread case with apple purée. Use more butter-dipped bread slices to make a lid. Bake the charlotte for 15 minutes, then lower heat to 180°C (350°F/Gas 4) and bake for 45 minutes more.

4 Cool the charlotte for 15 minutes before removing it from the tin. Serve hot, with cream.

Serves 6

Rhubarb Crumble

500g (1lb) rhubarb, trimmed and cut into 2.5cm (1in) lengths

250g (8oz) caster sugar

3 tblspn cornflour

60ml (2fl oz) water

125g (4oz) plain flour

pinch salt

45g (1½oz) butter, cubed

1 Preheat oven to 180°C (350°F/ Gas 4). Put the rhubarb in a saucepan with just enough water to cover. Add 185g (6oz) of the sugar and simmer, stirring occasionally, until tender.

2 Dissolve the cornflour in the measured water in a cup. Gradually add the mixture to the rhubarb, stirring constantly. Cook for 3 minutes more, stirring, then divide the rhubarb mixture between four ramekins.

3 Combine the flour and salt in a bowl. Rub in the butter until the mixture resembles breadcrumbs. Stir in the remaining sugar.

4 Spoon the topping over the rhubarb. Bake the crumbles for 20 minutes or until the topping on each is golden and crisp. Serve with whipped cream, crème fraîche or Greek yogurt, dusted with cinnamon, if liked.

Serves 4

Rhubarb Crumble

Apple and Blackberry Crumble Pie

Apple and Blackberry Crumble Pie

Pastry

220g (7oz) plain flour

100g (3¹/₂oz) caster sugar

100g (3¹/₂oz) butter, cubed

1 egg yolk

Filling

3 Bramley apples, peeled and sliced

2 eggs

125g (4oz) caster sugar

2 tblspn single cream

90g (3oz) ground almonds

250g (8oz) blackberries

Crumble

220g (7oz) plain flour

100g (3¹/₂oz) soft brown sugar

155g (5oz) butter, cubed

1 Preheat oven to 180°C (350°F/ Gas 4). Combine flour and sugar in a large bowl. Rub in butter until mixture resembles coarse breadcrumbs. Stir in egg yolk with enough iced water to bind. Alternatively, make the pastry in a food processor. Wrap pastry and chill for 20 minutes.

2 Roll out dough to line a deep 23cm (9in) flan dish with a removable base. Prick dough and bake for 10 minutes. Lower heat to 150°C (300°F/Gas 2).

3 Make filling. Poach apples in a saucepan of simmering water for 5 minutes; drain and cool. Arrange on the base of flan shell. Beat eggs, sugar, cream and almonds together and pour over apples. Scatter with blackberries.

4 Place crumble ingredients in a food processor and process until mixture resembles fine breadcrumbs. Sprinkle over pie and bake for 1 hour.

Serves 6-8

Lemon Pancakes

finely grated rind and juice of 2 lemons

125g (4oz) plain flour

60g (2oz) caster sugar

300ml (10fl oz) milk

1 egg

30g (1oz) butter, melted

1 Combine lemon rind, flour and sugar in a bowl. Make a well in centre. Mix lemon juice, milk and egg together; beat well. Slowly pour liquid into dry ingredients to make a batter; strain it, if necessary, to remove any lumps. Stir in half the melted butter.

2 Heat a pancake pan over moderately high heat, brush with a little butter and pour in just enough batter to coat base of pan. When golden on one side, flip pancake over and cook other side briefly. Keep hot while making seven more pancakes. Serve pancakes with lemon curd and cream, if liked.

Makes 8

Useful Information

Length

Centimetres	Inches	Centimetres	Inches
0.5 (5mm)	$1/4$	18	7
1	$1/2$	20	8
2	$3/4$	23	9
2.5	1	25	10
4	$1^1/_2$	30	12
5	2	35	14
6	$2^1/_2$	40	16
7.5	3	45	18
10	4	50	20
15	6	NB: 1cm = 10mm	

Metric/Imperial Conversion Chart
Mass (Weight)
(Approximate conversions for cookery purposes)

Metric	Imperial	Metric	Imperial
15g	$1/2$oz	315g	10oz
30g	1oz	350g	11oz
60g	2oz	375g	12oz ($3/4$lb)
90g	3oz	410g	13oz
125g	4oz ($1/4$lb)	440g	14oz
155g	5oz	470g	15oz
185g	6oz	500g (0.5kg)	16oz (1lb)
220g	7oz	750g	24oz ($1^1/_2$lb)
250g	8oz ($1/2$lb)	1000g (1kg)	32oz (2lb)
280g	9oz	1500 (1.5kg)	3lb

Metric Spoon Sizes

$1/4$ teaspoon = 1.25ml	
$1/2$ teaspoon = 2.5ml	
1 teaspoon = 5ml	
1 tablespoon =15ml	

Liquids

Metric	Imperial
30ml	1fl oz
60ml	2fl oz
90ml	3fl oz
125ml	4fl oz
155ml	5fl oz ($1/4$pt)
185ml	6fl oz
250ml	8fl oz
500ml	16fl oz
600ml	20fl oz (1pt)
750ml	$1^1/_4$pt
1 litre	$1^3/_4$pt
1.2 litres	2pt
1.5 litres	$2^1/_2$pt
1.8 litres	3pt
2 litres	$3^1/_2$pt
2.5 litres	4pt

Index

Editorial Coordination: Merehurst Limited
Cookery Editor: Jenni Fleetwood
Editorial Assistant: Sheridan Packer
Production Managers: Sheridan Carter, Anna Maguire
Layout and Finished Art: Stephen Joesph
Cover Photography: David Gill
Cover Design: Maggie Aldred
Cover Home Economist: Liz Trigg
Cover Sylist: Hilary Guy

Published by J.B. Fairfax Press Pty Limited
80-82 McLachlan Avenue
Rushcutters Bay 2011
A.C.N. 003 738 430

Formatted by J.B. Fairfax Press Pty. Ltd.
Printed by Toppan Printing Co, Singapore

JBFP 319 A/UK
Includes Index
ISBN 1 86343 116 0 (set)
ISBN 1 86343 158 6

Distribution and Sales Enquiries
Australia: J.B. Fairfax Press Pty Limited
Ph: (02) 361 6366 Fax: (02) 360 6262
United Kingdom: J.B. Fairfax Press Limited
Ph: (0933) 402330 Fax: (0933) 402234